Endorsements

"Few experiences can be lonelier for a man than the experience of miscarriage. I'm so thankful that in this brief book Eric Schumacher comes alongside grieving men to comfort, equip, and befriend them through their loss."
— **Tim Challies,** author of *Seasons of Sorrow*

"With courageous transparency, careful wording, and deep love, my dear brother Eric invites men into the confusion, loss, and shame that the death of an unborn child may bring. With a focus on honest testimony and faith in Jesus, he offers guidance to men who wonder, 'What do I do now?'"
— **Elyse Fitzpatrick,** author of *Because He Loves Me*

"Honest. Gut-wrenching. Hopeful. This book gives voice to a pain so many men carry in silence, and gently reminds them that Jesus still meets them there."
— **Jerrad Lopes,** founder of Dad Tired

"Honest, accessible, helpful, and mercifully brief. *Dads Hurt Too* offers the bereaved father the hope and companionship he needs in the wake of miscarriage in a format that he is able to digest amid the demands of his life and needs of his wife. This little book can be consumed in a single sitting, but the truths and perspective contained within it will transform a dad's entire journey through the grief of pregnancy loss."
— **Abbey Wedgeworth,** author, *Held: 31 Biblical Reflections on God's Comfort and Care in the Sorrow of Miscarriage*

"Losing a baby is a heartbreaking tragedy. Too often a father's grief goes unnoticed. Eric writes as a dad who knows this pain firsthand, offering the gospel hope with tenderness and grace."
— **Kristin Schmucker**, Co-Founder of The Daily Grace Co.

"Eric gives voice to a grief many fathers carry but few have ever dared to speak. With raw honesty and gospel-rooted hope, he invites us into sacred sorrow—and points us to a Savior who enters it with us. Every grieving dad needs this book, as does every person who wants to walk faithfully beside them."
— **Davey Blackburn,** founder, Nothing is Wasted Ministries

"Eric shares vulnerably about his experience: the numbness, the grief, and the desire to be strong while feeling ashamed of falling apart. A closing reflection from his wife offers a moving glimpse of the same loss through her eyes. This book is an invaluable resource—for helping men and women know they're not alone, and for equipping the church to care well after the pain of miscarriage."
— **Vaneetha Risner**, author of *Walking through Fire*

"There are no trite words here. A kind of mending tends each syllable. Each sentence is candle light. Each paragraph a companion. Each page whispered love. This is a book with healing in it. A healing hard-fought-for and grace-given. As a pastor, I'm grateful to have Eric and Jenny's gift to us, as a help to those I serve."
— **Zack Eswine,** author of *Spurgeon's Sorrows*

"…gives voice to some of the distressing thoughts and emotions that can arise in the wake of miscarriage. As Eric stewards his story of recurring loss for the benefit of others, he humbly shares the comforts of Christ in meaningful and relevant ways. I especially appreciated the opportunity to hear both a father's and a mother's perspective. This unique dynamic offers us a glimpse into the private—and sometimes *secret*—pain that parents endure when life is lost in the womb."
— **Christine M. Chappell,** certified biblical counselor; author *Midnight Mercies* and *Postpartum Depression*

"Honest, thoughtful, transparent, beautiful, and hopeful is the little book you hold in your hands. There is no better voice I know to give words to the unique burden a father feels when a child is lost in the womb than Eric's crucial voice in this space. I wish I had this resource when my wife and I lost a baby at 8 weeks many years ago, and I was lost to know how to feel and what to do. Read this book and know you are seen, loved, and your grief matters."
— **Brian Croft,** Executive Director, Practical Shepherding

"Eric's candid concerns and layers of grief are processed through the lens of truth and love. This book will leave readers with a greater appreciation of how Christ meets them in their dark hour of loss."
— **Emily Jensen,** author of *He Is Strong* and *Risen Motherhood*

"In *Dads Hurt Too*, my friend Eric Schumacher shares his heart-wrenching experiences with miscarriage. This is so much more than a self-help book for grieving fathers. Eric describes in vivid detail both the raw emotions and practical realities that men face, while providing a fresh voice of understanding that commends the comfort of Christ in the complexities of our grief. Soulful and necessary."
— **Ronnie Martin,** Director of Leader Care and Renewal for Harbor Network; author of *In the Morning You Hear My Voice*

"I love Eric's book. I mourned as I read, remembering our own miscarriages. And as I did, my heart also rejoiced. 'In his death, death died.' Our hope—a mother's and a father's hope—is a person, one who grieves with us, roars over death, and reigns to do something about it. If you have lost a baby, Eric's testimony will be a balm to your aching heart."
— **Kristen Wetherell,** coauthor of *Hope When It Hurts*

"I admire the courage, sensitivity, and patient hope with which Eric shares his family's grief. Fathers, grief after miscarriage isn't just important for your wife. You need to grieve and your wife needs you to join her in her grief. In *Dads Hurt Too*, Eric gives you a male voice, perspective, and model for grieving in a healthy way that leans into your faith and displays emotional leadership for your family."

— **Brad Hambrick,** Pastor of Counseling, The Summit Church

"Eric pulls back the curtain on the uncharted territory of a man's experience of miscarriage. In telling his story, he upholds the *imago dei* of babies lost to miscarriage, validates the grief of fathers, gives wives a glimpse into the struggles their husband may be facing, and frees men to grieve the loss of their child."

— **Brittany Allen**, author of *Lost Gifts: Miscarriage, Grief, and the God of All Comfort*

"The Schumachers' memoir is a gem for the brokenhearted. We highly recommend this hope-filled work not only for those who have experienced miscarriage, but for anyone who desires a tender and sacred look at how our Good Shepherd carries and comforts us in our sufferings."

— **Robert & Karen Cheong,** Gospel Care Ministries, author of *Restoration Story: Why Jesus Matters in a Broken World*

"Eric provides an opportunity for men to begin processing their pain as he vulnerably shares his honest, innermost thoughts as a father navigating the grief and trauma of four separate and unique miscarriages. Emboldened with the hope of the gospel, Eric opens the door for his brothers helping them to usher out comparison, shame, culture-biases, and loneliness and experience healing and wholeness in Christ."

— **Jessika Sanders**, Director, Praying Through Ministries

"Eric Schumacher has blessed the church with a priceless and much-needed gift by sharing a father's raw grief with miscarriage. This book affirms that dads also suffer during these agonizing times. Schumacher opens the door to his heart and gently invites us in to see his sorrow and Jesus more clearly in the dark valleys of the shadow of death. We are reminded that Jesus is with us in our confusing and painful moments. This book is a refreshingly honest look at a dad's suffering in miscarriage and is a helpful encouragement for hurting dads and those who walk alongside them. No matter your experience, read it devotionally and share it with others."
— **Dave Furman**, Chancellor, Gulf Theological Seminary; author of *Being There* and *Embracing God in Your Suffering*

"This book is a gift, not just to grieving fathers, but to anyone who has ever loved someone through loss. With tender honesty and striking insight, it gives voice to the often-overlooked pain of dads walking through miscarriage. Whether you're a mother, father, friend, or pastor, these pages will move you, equip you, and open your eyes to the quiet ache many carry. In exposing how the enemy compounds grief through isolation, accusation, and silence, Eric offers both gospel truth and hope. Every line feels personal because it is. It is hard, honest, and hopeful and that's exactly why everyone should read it."
— **Eliza Huie**, counselor; author of *Trauma Aware*

"*Dads Hurt Too* offers a beautiful glimpse into the heart of a father in a way that many men will relate to, and that may also give wives a clearer understanding of their husbands' deep grief and deep love. The dual perspective of Eric and Jenny beautifully illustrates how husbands and wives complement one another in loss, even as they experience sorrow in their own unique ways."
— **Kristin Hernandez**, host of the Hope Mommies podcast

DADS HURT TOO:
A FATHER'S MEMOIR OF MISCARRIAGE

Eric M. Schumacher

with an appendix by Jenny Schumacher —
Until Then: Trusting God Through Grief

© 2025 Eric M. Schumacher

ISBN: 978-1-7364080-3-2

All rights reserved. No part of this publication may be reproduced, distributed, or transmitted in any form or by any means, including photocopying, recording, or other electronic or mechanical methods, without the prior written permission of the publisher, except in the case of brief quotations embodied in critical reviews and certain other noncommercial uses permitted by copyright law.

Unless otherwise indicated, Scripture quotations marked CSB have been taken from the Christian Standard Bible®, Copyright © 2017 by Holman Bible Publishers. Used by permission. Christian Standard Bible® and CSB® are federally registered trademarks of Holman Bible Publishers.

Visit us on the web at emschumacher.com.

For the children we never met.
We love you.

Contents

Foreword	13
Introduction	21
Dads Hurt Too	25
Appendix: Until Then	63
For Further Reading	83
Acknowledgements	85

Foreword

After reading *Dads Hurt Too*, my heart is filled with so many things. I am reminded that we live in a broken, fallen, and groaning world, where suffering is a universal human experience. If you are not suffering now, you will someday, and if you are not suffering now, you are near someone who is. In this world of suffering, death still haunts us, with its searing pain and indescribable loss. I am reminded that death is often accompanied by deafening silence. The loved ones of the deceased hide in their grief, not sure of how to respond the right way, not sure of what to say, and not wanting to talk even if they knew what to say. The community around them is also often afraid to speak, fearful of saying the wrong thing, so they often opt for silence. This reminds me of why it is such a blessing for Eric Schumacher, on behalf of countless men, to break the silence, with shocking transparency and humility. Men suffer too, often in lonely confusion and shame.

I am reminded that suffering is spiritual warfare, and even more so, suffering the death of one who didn't even have a chance to live. I am reminded that suffering is never a neutral experience, because we never come to our suffering empty-handed. We carry our previous experiences, long-ago-formed assumptions, our functional theology, what other people have told us, and a host of other things to our pain and loss. These shape the way we interpret and understand what we are going through. Often we are pulled between bad thinking, the devil's lies, and remnants of the awareness of God's presence, his sovereignty, and his grace, while we just wish this were all a bad dream. In the middle of this spiritual war, it often feels like there is no one who will come alongside and fight with us.

I am also reminded that these dramatic moments of death, loss, and pain are not often moments of courage and self-confidence. As much as you prepare yourself for what could happen, you never feel prepared when it does happen. We are not sure what to say and do. We question our feelings, and then question our questions. We finally make a choice, only to revisit it again and again, wondering if we did the right thing. We feel unsure, exposed, sometimes misunderstood, and judged. It's like walking up the stairs with numb feet. We're dragging ourselves up, but each step is unsure.

I am reminded that in these moments everyone proves to be a theologian, a philosopher, and an archeologist. We don't just respond based on the facts of our present experience, but based on our interpretation of those facts. We dig into the mound of our past experiences, trying to make sense out of the present. And in our grief, we will always preach some kind of gospel to ourselves. It is either a false gospel of a God who is distant, uncaring, and uninvolved, and of a universe that is unfair, or we speak to ourselves of the true gospel of Jesus Christ with the hope that is found in his presence, power, promises, and inexhaustible grace.

As I read my way through Eric's experience, there was one passage that kept coming to mind. It was written about one of the darkest and seemingly most hopeless periods of suffering recorded in the Bible. Israel had been enslaved in Egypt for over four hundred years. Can you imagine? Did anyone see their long travail? Did anyone hear their cries? Did anyone know and understand what they were going through? Did anyone remember them? The answer to these questions is recorded and preserved for us in Exodus 2:24-25 because God loves us: "And God heard their groaning, and God remembered his covenant with Abraham, with Isaac, and with Jacob. God saw the people of Israel—and God knew."

Here are four wonderful words of hope that I have clung to in my own seasons of suffering. God *hears* your cries. God *remembers* you and the promises he has made to you. God *sees* every aspect of your pain, every moment of your grief, and every instance of your confusion. And God *knows*, to the very depths of your heart, what you are going through. Jesus lived, died, rose again, and ascended so that this God would be your Father forever. These words remind us that in the loss and pain of miscarriage, hope is a person, and his name is Jesus.

I am both grieved and excited that you have this book in your hands. Grieved that having this book means you are facing the unwanted, the unplanned, and the unthinkable. But I am excited that there is a humble, God-fearing, Scripture-informed, and gospel-loving brother who has walked before you and who has been willing to bear his soul so that you may find comfort and hope in your moment of loss. Read this little book with an open heart. You will be glad you did.

Paul David Tripp
August 8, 2025

Introduction

It grieves me that you're holding this book. The fact that you've opened it suggests that you—or a man you love—has lost a child he never got the chance to hold.

For many men, miscarriage is a lonely and silent journey. They haven't heard other men speak about pregnancy loss. They wonder if they're allowed to hurt, to weep, to speak, to grieve—so they bury the pain, stifle the tears, and silence the questions, remaining alone in their sorrow.

This little book is my attempt to break that silence and end that solitude.

This book is my story. It's not a how-to guide or a manual on grief. It's not a theology textbook or a Bible study. It's a glimpse into my heart and mind as I walked through four miscarriages as a father—an exploration of my trials and the comfort I found in Christ.

This book is an invitation to speak. May bereaved fathers be empowered to explore their losses and share their stories. May family and friends leave these pages better equipped to listen and respond in love.

Ultimately, this book is an offer of hope. Even when I felt otherwise, I was never alone. In every loss, I found Jesus a faithful companion, a sympathetic listener, a partner in pain, and a gentle friend. I pray you find him to be the same.

At the end of the book, I've included a short piece written by my wife, Jenny. It offers a window into a mother's grief—a voice fathers need to hear. I include it not to shift the focus but to help us understand the women who walk with us through this pain.

Our essays were previously published online. Jenny posted hers on Valentine's Day, 2011, after the burial of our third miscarried child. Mine was first published February 2019, at *Risen Motherhood*, several years after our fourth and final miscarriage. Aside from light editing, both pieces remain essentially unchanged, preserving the voice, tone, and emotional honesty of those early moments as they were experienced and expressed at the time.

A few years ago, I had the opportunity to write a 31-day devotional titled *Ours: Biblical Comfort for Men Grieving Miscarriage*. It addresses many of the questions fathers face in the wake of pregnancy loss. When you're ready to go deeper into that journey, I pray it serves you well.

Thank you for choosing to hear our story. Jenny and I are honored to be a part of yours now. As you read, we pray the grace of God the Father comforts you through the knowledge of Jesus Christ in the power of his Holy Spirit.

Eric Schumacher

Dads Hurt Too:
A Father's Memoir
of Miscarriage

"Catch the foxes for us —
the little foxes that ruin the vineyards."
— Song of Songs 2:15

My wife and I have nine children, but if you meet us, we'll only say we have five. That's because we've only ever named five—the five we've met, the five who took breaths, the five we brought home. Four of our children died by "miscarriage."

Medically speaking, miscarriage is the spontaneous loss of a pregnancy within the first 20 weeks of gestation; it is the death of a baby in the womb. As with most suffering I did not expect to experience it personally;

miscarriage happened to other people. I certainly never considered it from the father's perspective. Miscarriage seemed to be—before it happened to us—solely a woman's experience, a mother's sorrow. Now I know differently. Moms hurt, and dads hurt too.

I don't share my experience with miscarriage as definitive, as though I speak for every father. Each person's experience with miscarriage is unique. This is mine. I share it with two hopes: First, to free other fathers to speak, to grieve, and to heal. Second, to help miscarrying mothers begin to understand and know how to relate to their partners in the midst of this painful loss.

In my experience with miscarriage, I encountered four "little foxes" in the vineyard of grief, unwelcome pests that gnawed on the vine of sorrow so that it would not blossom and bear good fruit. This is my story.

The First Fox — Comparison
Despite arriving pale, blue, and breathless—the umbilical cord cinching a death grip on his throat—our first child lived, as did our second and our third.

We first experienced the death of a child in the womb in September 2007, a year after the birth of Living Child #3. We lost the baby early in the unannounced pregnancy, at only four and a half weeks. The bleeding started the day after a home pregnancy test. Had she not taken it, we might have thought her cycle had simply started late.

Around the same time, close family members lost their baby in an emergency procedure for a painful and life-threatening ectopic pregnancy. Another family member miscarried a baby several weeks further along than ours.

We discussed it and chose silence. We told no one. We feared drawing attention away from their loss onto ours. Others were suffering "worse" than we were. After all, how did the uncomplicated and almost unnoticed loss of an unexpected and unannounced pregnancy compare to their painful and public suffering? They "deserved" the sympathy and support more than we did.

And there it was, that first little fox in the vineyard of grief—comparison. A ruthless enemy, comparison is quick to use your family, your wife, your children, and your friends against you.

Comparison sank its teeth in deeper with each of the three subsequent miscarriages, further stifling my grief. I had not carried these children. I had not undergone a dilation and curettage (D&C), a doctor scraping the body of my child out of my own. I had not endured contractions, laboring to deliver a dead baby. I had not been whisked to the operating room over concerns of excessive blood loss. My wife had. She suffered. What was my experience compared to hers? Who was I to mourn?

Comparison pointed a paw at our living children—three of them, then four, then five—and demanded, "What right have you to mourn a child you never knew, when you have all these?" Comparison thrust the faces of friends before my own—friends who could not conceive, friends without a living child, friends whose children died in the crib or in college—and mocked, "You mourn, but not as those who have no kids. Others are worse off; stifle your sorrow."

A Better Word
The gospel speaks a better word than the bark of comparison. It speaks of a Father who notices and values the minutia of his world—even the parts that others deem worthless by comparison.

"Aren't two sparrows sold for a penny? Yet not one of them falls to the ground without your Father's consent. But even the hairs of your head have all been counted," Jesus assures us. "So don't be afraid; you are worth more than many sparrows" (Matthew 10:29-31). The argument here is not: people matter, and therefore sparrows are insignificant. Rather: sparrows are significant, so how much more valuable are those created in God's image?

God's voice—not the voices in my head or that of my neighbors—is the final word on the matter: If he values the hairs of my head more than sparrows, how much more must he care for my child—his own image bearer? And when that child falls to sleep, hidden in my wife's womb, will the Father in heaven not notice the father on earth? God cares for these little ones. God cares about mothers. God cares about fathers. Both moms and dads have every right to mourn.

The Second Fox — Shame

Our daughter—Living Child #4—entered the world in December 2008 with no complications. In the spring of 2010, we learned another baby was on its way, due in February 2011. On a family vacation in July, my wife experienced strange contraction pains. We saw her doctor when we returned.

The ultrasound technician didn't deliver the news; she said the doctor would be in shortly to explain what we saw on the screen. His explanation wasn't necessary. The image of that still, peanut-shaped body, settled at the bottom of her uterus told us all we needed to know. As my wife wiped cold ultrasound gel from her stomach and hot tears from her cheeks, the fact settled on us—the baby had died. Miscarriage #2.

We waited a week, hoping the baby's body would pass "naturally." When it did not, the doctor ordered a D&C.

The doctor—the most compassionate physician we've known—invited me to sit next to my wife during the procedure. I'd watched the full process of childbirth four times, without queasiness or flinching. As a pastor, I'd witnessed some gruesome things in emergency rooms and at hospital bedsides. Yet, I could not bring myself to sit next to my wife as this happened. I opted to sit against the wall, behind her. Even then, as the doctor made preparations, anxiety, nausea, dizziness crept up from my gut, through my chest, and into my head. I told her that I couldn't stay and exited to the waiting room.

I found a chair in an empty area, hoping to avoid seeing and being seen by others. My strategy failed. A chatty guest took a seat next to me and started a conversation.

"You call yourself a husband? What kind of husband leaves—no—*abandons* his wife in the midst of her suffering and makes her endure it alone?" it barked. "What kind of pathetic wimp can't even hold his wife's hand while she goes through this? You call yourself a man? You're a loser."

I recognized the voice. The craftiest of the foxes, shame darts in and out, appearing in the most unexpected of situations. It had gnawed on me before, chiding me for my inability to help my wife, to give input and counsel on decisions pertaining to the particulars of women's health that I simply did not understand. Now shame insisted that I had failed—failed myself, failed my wife, failed my God.

Late that fall we received good news: another baby was on the way. Cautious, due to the previous miscarriage, we waited to tell our children until we heard the heartbeat. As the pregnancy progressed, so did our optimism. The anticipation of meeting this child would carry past February 10, the due date of the previous one.

On February 7, 16 weeks pregnant, my wife saw her doctor with a few concerns. The ultrasound confirmed the baby had died. The doctor presented the options of another D&C or inducing labor. To avoid the risks of the former, we chose the latter.

Plus, the doctor suggested that we would be able to hold the baby after delivery, something we both desired.

Two days later, my wife was induced. At 4:40 p.m., turned on her side, she felt a gush of fluid. Our 4.5-inch, 0.8-ounce baby was born. We were alone, the three of us.

I saw the baby, lying there on the bed, wet with blood and amniotic fluid. My fatherly instinct told me to pick up my child, to cradle its fragile body, to not let it lie there alone. But I didn't. I didn't know if I was allowed. Shame whispered in my ear, "What will the nurses say if they find you holding the baby? Won't they think that odd?" So, instead, I pressed the nurse-call button and explained what happened.

As we waited for the nurse, the same voice that discouraged me from holding the baby now chastised me for letting it lie, "Look at your baby, lying there helpless and alone. What kind of a father just lets his baby lie there?"

The nurses arrived, attended to my wife, and took the baby. The doctor arrived. Concerned about a stubborn placenta and excessive blood loss, he rushed her to the operating room for a D&C, the very procedure we hoped to avoid. I waited alone, frightened and ashamed.

In the morning, as she recovered her strength and we prepared to go home, we asked to see the baby. Shame told me this was foolish, that the nurses thought we were crazy for wanting this, that they were probably rolling their eyes and shaking their heads.

A dear friend, a nurse who happened to be on duty, brought the baby to us and gently explained that our child might not look as we expected. The soft, underdeveloped skeletal structure collapses as the fluids dry. We understood. We cradled the little blanket in our hands, unfolding its edges to reveal our little one—eyes still fused shut, a delicate nose and dainty mouth. We touched skinny arms and legs, counting perfect fingers and toes.

When we had finished viewing our baby, I called the nurses' station to ask if someone could come take the baby back. A nurse, apparently unaware of our situation, explained that all the nurses were busy. She asked if there were a reason we didn't want to keep the baby in the room. "Our baby...," I stuttered. I didn't know what the proper term was for this situation. Miscarried? Stillbirth? I finally finished, "...was born dead."

Shame whispered, "You're such a nuisance. They have real, living babies to take care of and now she has to leave them to tend to you. She probably thinks you're an idiot."

The head nurse, a compassionate woman, made efforts to accommodate our circumstances before we arrived. She arranged a room on a wing with no other patients. My wife would not have to pass the nursery or rooms with balloons and "Congratulations" signs on the doors on her way in or out. A single rose taped to the doorframe explained our situation to entering nurses. But the process did not seem to consider the father.

This hospital only issued identification bands to patients—that is, mothers and living babies—and to the fathers of living children. This meant that when I left the maternity ward to meet a visiting pastor or took a walk down the hall, I couldn't simply walk back to our room. I had to explain to the ever-rotating desk staff who I was and why I was there. Sometimes they made me wait at the door of the maternity ward while they called my wife to confirm I could go to the room. As I stood there, suspect in the eyes of new staff and a curiosity to people in the waiting room, shame nipped at my heels.

Meals were delivered to the rooms for mothers. Fathers could go to a hospitality room in the maternity ward to fill a tray from a hot buffet during set hours. This meant that all the fathers in the ward gathered in the small room at once, making small talk as they waited in line.

Guess what fathers small talk about in a maternity ward. "So, what did you have?" "Is your wife in labor or has she delivered?" "You want to see a picture?" Getting food meant bringing my sorrow into a stranger's joy, which meant more barks from shame. "Look at these smiling men, excited to talk about their babies. You're such a downer."

We left the hospital on February 10, the due date of the previous baby, our hearts doubly empty. When you walk beside your wife's wheelchair as the nurse pushes her from the room to the front door of the hospital, people pay attention. Smiling staff stand to peek over the desk to see the little one in the new mother's arms. My wife carried a potted plant and a sympathy card. Shame told me what a disappointment we were, a dark cloud in this bright place.

That next Monday, a sunny and warm Valentine's Day, our whole family gathered around a little gravesite, where I read Revelation 21:1-5 and prayed, before leaving our child to be buried. Even making these arrangements brought shame. "They probably think this is ridiculous and can't wait for you to let them get back to real work."

Jesus Wept

How does a father trap and kill this little fox—the voice of shame, using miscarriage to tell him he's but a weakling, a failure, and a nuisance? It's not by "manning up" and "toughing it out." It's not by crawling into a hole and hiding in silence. What a hurting dad needs is to hear that there is one who sees and knows and is not ashamed to call him brother.

"Jesus wept" (John 11:35). He stood at the tomb of Lazarus and cried. Jesus, the one through whom God created the universe, stood at his friend's grave and sobbed. Overwhelmed with the real experience of grief and loss, Jesus wept.

Those two words summarize so much of what the Bible tells us about God. He is the God who heard the cries of the Israelites in slavery, who saw, and who knew. In Jesus, this God became flesh and dwelt among us, experiencing our sadness.

To be our Savior, it was necessary for him to suffer. He was a man of sorrows and acquainted with grief. He hungered. He thirsted. He grew tired. He told his friends, "I am deeply grieved to the point of death," asking them to "remain here and stay awake with me" (Matthew 26:38)—only to weep alone while they slept. He grew so physically weak that another man had to carry his cross to Golgotha. He died for us so that through his resurrection we might live.

The road to resurrection does not follow the path of strength and convenience. We, like Jesus, are "made perfect through suffering." That is how the Father brings his sons and daughters to glory. Therefore, Jesus is not ashamed to call us brothers and sisters (see Hebrews 2:10-11).

Does shame point out my sin? "But he was pierced because of our rebellion, crushed because of our iniquities; punishment for our peace was on him, and we are healed by his wounds." (Isaiah 53:5).

Does shame point out my weakness? Jesus identifies with all my weakness. "He himself took our weaknesses" (Matthew 8:17).

Does shame say that I am an unwanted burden in my grief? "He protects his flock like a shepherd; he gathers the lambs in his arms and carries them in the fold of his garment" (Isaiah 40:11).

Does shame tell grieving fathers to hide their tear-streaked faces, that no one wants to associate with a frail sufferer? The Gospel speaks a better word: "Jesus is not ashamed to call them brothers" (Hebrews 2:11).

Jesus wept. You can too.

The Third Fox — Culture
The day we returned from the hospital, I headed to the store to fill a prescription for my wife. As I drove, I turned on the radio, set to my usual public radio channel. A state lawmaker and the host were discussing some bit of abortion legislation. The legislator quipped something like, "You know, it's not a big deal. We're only talking about fetuses up to 18-weeks." These words hit my heart like salt in a bite wound.

There it was, the little fox sent to choke out grief and stifle the growth of healthy mourning—our culture. We live in a culture where politicians can reduce my baby to an "only" for the sake of votes. Where corporations press the language of "no big deal" so that they can cut big deals trafficking the body parts we just buried. Where we fathers are denied entry into the conversation because we lack the proper anatomy.

How do we mourn what leaders label an "only" and a "no big deal"?

The Indignant Boy Who Lived

Christmas rebukes our culture. The nativity scene speaks hope to the grieving father.

"When Elizabeth heard Mary's greeting, the baby leaped inside her" (Luke

1:41). Not an "only." Not a "no big deal." A baby leaped inside her.

"This will be the sign for you: You will find a baby wrapped tightly in cloth and lying in a manger" (Luke 2:12). Not an "only." Not a "no big deal." A baby will be lying in the manger.

The same Greek word for baby is used in both verses, assuring us with divine authority that what is in the womb is every bit as much a baby as what is lying in the manger.

That swaddled baby faced a similar culture, one in which a lawmaker, driven by the desire to preserve his power and profit, would decree the child's death via the murder of all the young boys in Bethlehem. But that fox did not win.

The boy who lived grew to be a man who fought to the death for life. At Lazarus' tomb, Jesus witnessed his friends weeping as he approached the burial place of his friend. John twice records that he was "deeply moved" (John 11:33, 38), translated from a Greek word used to describe a horse snorting, which indicated being moved with indignation or anger. So we find Jesus, staring death in the face, full of indignation, snorting in anger at his enemy.

Dads and moms are right to be overcome with emotion in the face of death. Jesus joins them. Death—from the womb to the tomb—is a big deal. It is not an "only." It is an enemy, a foreign invader, smuggled in on the back of sin, wreaking havoc in our world. It should be stared down with snorting indignation.

Only let us entrust our indignation to the hands of our Warrior King. For while our anger cannot resolve the problem, Jesus' anger did. He demanded, "Lazarus, come out!" And the man who had died came out alive.

Not long after this, Jesus cried out again—"It is finished!"—as he succumbed to the wages of sin on our behalf. There, in his death, death died. And in his resurrection, he won the resurrection of his people—of all those who trust in him (and, I would argue, all the little ones we've lost in the womb). Fathers and mothers resist the culture of death by being firm in their faith in the Lord of Life.

The Fourth Fox — Loneliness

In God's kindness, we survived that year. Our son—Living Child #5—was born February 8, 2012, allowing us to spend the anniversary of our loss enjoying our newborn. With his birth, we were finished having children—miscarriage and the little foxes were not.

In December 2014, I accepted a call to be associate pastor at a new church. We packed and moved to a new city, to this new congregation, filled with new people.

We discovered in January that, despite our decision to be finished having children, my wife was pregnant. We hit a wall of conflicting emotions. Pregnancy had grown increasingly burdensome and destructive to her body, especially in the summer heat. We hadn't wanted another child. Yet, we treasure children. We knew we should want this child.

It didn't take long for our hearts to change. We grew excited about the baby; we wanted this. No sooner did our hearts warm to the reality of a new baby than the baby was gone, miscarried at 5 weeks.

Waves of grief and emotion crashed over us. Grief over feeling grief at the news of the pregnancy. Grief over losing a baby that we now wanted. Relief at avoiding a painful and hard pregnancy. Guilt over feeling relieved. Shame had a field day. "What kind of a parent doesn't want a baby? Who feels relief at a baby's death?"

Shame didn't arrive alone. The old fox brought a new friend to the party—loneliness. And she arrived with a whole litter of pups.

We hadn't told family about the pregnancy yet; it was too soon. Shame whispered, "Can't you hear them now: 'Don't you know what causes that?' 'Weren't you being careful?' 'Ah, well, at least you have those five! No big deal!'" So, we said nothing and suffered alone.

At our previous church, a community of people we'd known and loved for years, loneliness had been my companion in miscarriage. The Sunday following miscarriage #3, most of the women talked to my wife offering sympathy; friends attended to her. I only remember one or two men giving me a hug. One met me at the door, waiting for me. His infant son had died in his arms on Christmas Day a decade before. Other than those, while a few men may have asked how she was doing or offered a quick "we're praying for you," I can't recall anyone asking how I was doing. Burnt out from several years of church conflict, I was in no shape to ask for help. I don't recall anyone following up with me in the weeks that followed. (I admit my memory may have failed, and I ask forgiveness of any sympathizers I've forgotten.) I don't blame them; I'm certainly not bitter. I'm guilty of the same response. Too often, I've awkwardly avoided or simply overlooked such suffering brothers. We just don't know how to deal with it, if we notice at all.

But now we were in a new church, full of new people, too new to have any close, time-tested friendships. So, while my wife confided in a few, I stayed silent. Shame whispered, "They didn't hire you so that they could carry your sorrows. You're here to carry theirs. If you share this, you'll just be a disappointing nuisance." This wasn't true, of course. But shame is never one to let the facts stand in the way of an accusation.

The loneliness multiplies. How can I talk to my wife about my loss? Loneliness. How do we mourn the anniversaries of loss in a community of people that never met the one who's missing? Loneliness. What's a man to do?

You Are Not Alone
"I am with you always" (Matthew 28:20). This is Jesus' promise to his disciples in this world. A promise he kept when he poured out his Holy Spirit at Pentecost. A promise he keeps as his Spirit dwells in our hearts through faith.

In the midst of my darkest shame, Jesus dwells in me.

In the midst of grief too deep for words, the Spirit intercedes on my behalf.

In the midst of a hostile culture, Jesus is with me.

In the midst of unthoughtful words, Jesus hears and sees and knows.

Fathers, as we trust that the Spirit of God dwells within us individually, we must also believe that Jesus dwells in his body corporately—specifically in the local church. Christ indwells all his people and, through them, ministers to us.

There is much grace to be found going to church. Listen to the congregation sing the gospel, pray to a listening Father, and confess the faith. Hear the Good News declared as the word is read and preached.

Watch a baptism, take the Lord's Supper, and remember that Jesus died for you and rose from the dead.

Foxes Still Bark – The Lion Still Roars

It's been almost three years since our last miscarriage. Wounds are healing. Yet, I'd be lying if I said those foxes don't still bark and nip from time to time.

Even as I write this, those foxes run circles around my chair, barking for attention: Will I be rebuked for speaking of my own suffering when others have suffered more? Accused of downplaying how mothers suffer by highlighting a father's pain? Will I be whispered about in secret for the ways I've failed? Ridiculed for mourning a person who was never born? What if someone takes offense, thinking I'm calling them out in some way? What if people use past weakness to form future accusation? Perhaps I should delete this now and stay silent and alone?

But those voices won't win. Jesus, the Lion of Judah, roars louder than the foxes. Over the years, he has proved his promise, "My grace is sufficient for you, for my power is perfected in weakness" (2 Corinthians 12:9).

The accuser, who dispatched the foxes, is overthrown not by my silence, but by the Lamb of God who took away my sin and saves me by grace through faith in him.

Over the past decade, I've tried to be intentional in speaking of my afflictions—miscarriages, conflicts, weaknesses, depression, anxiety, failure, loss, and disappointment. I know there are men who simply don't understand. There are men who roll their eyes. But then there are those men who pull me aside at conferences, who drop me an email, who meet me for coffee, who call me and say in quiet tones, "We had a miscarriage. I don't know what to do. I know you've been through it. Could we talk?"

So we talk. I listen to their grief. I offer what little wisdom and practical tips I can. I speak of Jesus, the Son who roared in the face of death and crushed its head. Then we ask the Father who hears and sees and knows to give us faith and hope and love.

It is with that hope that I publish these words—hope that grieving fathers and mothers might hear and find the freedom to speak, to grieve, to believe, to heal, and to live.

Until Then: Trusting God Through Grief

by Jenny Schumacher

written February 14, 2011

"Look, I am making everything new."
— Revelation 21:5

A week ago on Monday at 10:00 a.m., I saw our little baby for the first time via ultrasound. Today on Monday at 10:00 a.m., we buried that same child—on Valentine's Day.

Just a short week ago, I was 16 weeks pregnant, and in a whirlwind of a few short days, I found out the baby had died, and then I delivered the little one. Just as the bruises from the two failed IV attempts are fading and the tape marks from the successful one are wearing off,

JENNY SCHUMACHER

I know that the pain will ease over time—but now, it is still so close.

I went to the doctor last Monday with some concerns. I had noticed my uterus was softer, I could sleep on my stomach again, and some of my jeans were fitting more loosely. A couple days earlier I even laid on the floor and cried, fearing I was going to have to go through another miscarriage.

I told the doctor about my concerns. He said I was measuring right where he would expect. But then there was no heartbeat. Of the many, many heartbeat checks I've had over all my pregnancies, only one other time has the doctor been unable to find the heartbeat—and that wasn't good news either.

The doctor went to get the portable ultrasound, but when he turned it on, the baby wasn't moving and he couldn't find a heartbeat so he scheduled me for the big ultrasound machine a half hour later.

He kindly let me wait in the exam room, and even brought me his cell phone to call Eric, so I didn't have to call from the lobby. (I'm currently in the running for the last person in the States to have a cell phone).

The nurse came in after a bit and stayed with me a few minutes kindly offering her sympathy. I have to say that my doctor and his nurse are such compassionate people. I can imagine how the reality of so many miscarriages would desensitize you to your job, but they have been so compassionate through my three miscarriages. It was such a blessing to me.

One of the first thoughts I remember having after returning to the exam room was: "The Lord gives, and the Lord takes away. Blessed be the name of the Lord" (Job 1:21). I thank God for teaching me the truth of his sovereignty many years before he would walk me through this pain and trial. I can't imagine having been taught by my church that God wants me to have my best life now and then face this. I can't imagine having to give birth to my baby after it died and then be told that God wishes it wouldn't have happened but couldn't prevent it. I see no hope in those situations.

Has it made the grief any less? I'm not sure. The grief is still very real and very here, but the strength he gives me to make it through the grief comes from knowing that he is in control of the world and of all that happens. Nothing slips by his attention and he never makes a mistake. I am still grieved, but I am comforted to know that not only is God near to the broken-hearted but that he loves me and his plan is for my best no matter if I cannot clearly see it now, or maybe ever on this earth.

Eric arrived soon after I got back to the room, and then the doctor came in to talk to us. My doctor gave me the options of inducing or having a D&C. The risks of having a D&C at this point were not appealing, so I opted for induction even though it meant more pain and possibly a long hospital stay. He also said we would be able to hold the baby after it was born, which was a comforting thought.

Monday was a difficult day. Fresh was the wound of the baby dying, and we had logistics to take care of: call my mom to watch the kids Wednesday, arrange for her to take our oldest to the school office for his standardized tests on Wednesday through Friday mornings, plan for our hospital stay, and make plans with the funeral home for burial. We knew that after seeing and holding the baby it would be hard to just let them dispose of it with their medical waste.

Meanwhile, Tuesday morning, all of the kids had dental appointments and by the time we got home, our daughter was running a temp of 103°. That night it went up to 104.2° and wouldn't come down even with ibuprofen. She had the chills and her breathing rate was above normal so the nurse said we should take her into the ER to monitor her for respiratory distress. This was 7:30 p.m. the night before I was to be induced.

We decided not to take her into the ER. Her temperature did eventually come down and by 9:00 p.m. her breathing was normal. However, I had little sleep that night, waking up with her because her temperature had gone back up and her breathing had quickened again.

When we left for the hospital that morning, she was sleeping without a fever and breathing normally, but I had a difficult time leaving her, even in the good care of my parents. How do you leave your sick, sick little girl so you can go to the hospital to deliver a dead baby?

The staff at the hospital was very kind and helpful in letting us know what to expect. We had been in labor and delivery four times already, but we weren't sure in what ways this would be similar and different.

Around 10:00 a.m. the doctor finally got things started by using a couple different things to cause my cervix to dilate and to start my uterus contracting. Within the hour I started feeling kind of achy. They gave me Cytotec every three hours to cause contractions. By 1:40 p.m. I was contracting every 1–1.5 minutes. The nurse kept asking if I wanted anything for the pain, but I really wanted to be awake and not out of it when the baby was born. I had my last dose of Cytotec at 3:40 p.m.

When the doctor came in around 4:30 p.m. to check on me, I was at 4 centimeters. I figured that it was pretty good to go from

0 to 4 in 6.5 hours considering at 16 weeks the cervix has no intention of dilating. He broke the sac of water and the nurse said it wouldn't be too much longer.

About 4:40 p.m., I felt a strange feeling and a gush of fluid. Our baby was born February 9 at 4:43 p.m. and was 4.5 inches long, and weighed 0.8 ounces. My nurse said she couldn't tell the gender because it was just a little too early, but another nurse later labeled the baby as a girl.

The placenta wasn't so eager to depart, so after half an hour, the doctor thought I had lost enough blood and whisked me away to the OR for a D&C. Thus I still had to go through the procedure I wanted to avoid. The doctor assured us that the risks weren't as great since it was just the placenta he would be removing. Plus, the baby was born whole and we would eventually be able to see it, which again was comforting.

I returned to my room around 7:30 p.m., but was groggy most of the evening. We spent a not so restful night at the hospital and in the morning we were able to hold our baby. I knew that seeing our little one would be difficult, but I was afraid that I would always wonder what our little one looked like if I didn't. She was tiny, and weighed hardly anything. We could see the eyes that were still fused shut, the minuscule nose and tiny mouth. All the miniature fingers and toes were there, and arms and legs that were impossibly skinny.

While in the hospital there were several times that Eric had to explain why he was there and why he didn't have an ID band (they only give them to fathers after a baby is born, alive). It didn't bother us because we understood that our situation wasn't the norm, but we did feel bad for the people who had made assumptions that we had a baby in the nursery.

However, I was unprepared for the feelings I would have going home. I didn't expect how hard it would be to see our children who had once been as tiny as that little baby, but they had each grown into the children that they are. I praise God that they did grow! But at the same time, it was difficult knowing that this little one would never grow as they have and will continue to do.

Each day that has passed has brought different feelings and emotions. At first, I didn't want to face anyone. My emotions were too raw and too close. I dreaded going to church on Sunday because I was afraid that people would try to talk to me about it, though I knew that it would be worse if I saw them and they ignored my pain. Either way, it was going to hurt.

One thing I have learned through this grieving is that even if you can't imagine the pain someone is going through, it is best to communicate exactly that rather than ignore their grief. I appreciated one person's admission of, "I don't know what to say, but I'm praying for you" more than another person's response of silence. This is coming from someone who would previously have chosen silence over words when confronted with another person's pain.

This whole situation has been even more difficult because the baby we lost last summer was due on February 10, the day we left the hospital. So not only did I have to deliver a baby and not return home with it, but it was the day that we were supposed to be coming home with a lively little baby. And this summer when this baby would have been due, we'll still not be coming home with a little one.

Compounding this pain is the question whether or not we should have another baby. I have struggled with the sadness of wondering if we will ever bring another little one home from the hospital, if I'll ever carry another newborn in a sling, or if we'll ever make use of all the baby stuff we still have tucked away in the attic and basement.

JENNY SCHUMACHER

We long for another baby, but there is so much to consider.

When I got pregnant last summer, it had not been our plan to have another, but we were thrilled. Then the baby died. When I got pregnant again this fall we weren't intending for me to get pregnant, but I did and we were excited, especially because we had lost the baby that summer. We waited to tell the kids until after I had heard the heartbeat because we didn't want to go through the pain of telling them only to explain the baby had died. But of course, that is exactly what happened again.

This is the third miscarriage I've had and each has been progressively later in pregnancy. We don't want to go through this again, and each pregnancy makes my varicose veins more painful. Top that all off with the fact that I keep getting older.

I have felt great sorrow and grief through these trials, but I think the only "why" question I have had is, "God, why cause me to get pregnant twice when we weren't intending it only to end the pregnancies early?"

If we had been trying to get pregnant I might think God was saying that our childbearing years have come to an end. But why walk us through this grief? I may never know the answer to that question, but I am thankful that it has been God who has walked us through it and that he didn't leave us to walk alone.

God has also blessed us immensely through the body of Christ around us. We have received many cards, gifts, meals, phone calls and kind words. It has been encouraging to have others walk through this with us as they pray and minister to us.

So this morning instead of making my kids heart pancakes for breakfast and cutting out valentines for school, we bundled the kids into the car, our youngest boy in his 'funeral and cemetery shirt' as he called it.

We drove across town to the cemetery where our baby was to be buried. It was windy, but sunny and warm (for February). Eric read from Revelation 21:1-5, and he prayed. We left that little body there at the cemetery to be put in the ground until the day it will be raised up.

Until then, we trust that God has the soul of our little one with him in heaven and one day when we are called home we will get to hold our child in our arms once again, but this time alive.

> *Then I heard a loud voice from the throne: Look, God's dwelling is with humanity, and he will live with them. They will be his peoples, and God himself will be with them and will be their God. He will wipe away every tear from their eyes. Death will be no more; grief, crying, and pain will be no more, because the previous things have passed away.*
> *Then the one seated on the throne said, "Look, I am making everything new."*
>
> *— Revelation 21:3-5 —*

For Further Reading

Ours: Biblical Comfort for Men Grieving Miscarriage
by Eric M. Schumacher

*Held: 31 Biblical Reflections on God's Comfort
and Care in the Sorrow of Miscarriage*
by Abbey Wedgeworth

*In His Hands: Prayers for Your Child
or Baby in a Medical Crisis*
by Eric M. Schumacher & Jessika Sanders

For more resources from Eric M. Schumacher,
please visit emschumacher.com.

Acknowledgements

Jesus — Thank you for living, dying, rising, reigning, and soon returning, that we might share eternal life with you. Apart from you there is no hope in the face of death.

Jenny — Thank you for your faithful love and patient grace in this hard journey we call "life." Thank you also for your courage in sharing your story, that others might find hope and healing. I love you.

Emily Jensen — Thank you, friend, for inviting me to reflect on my journey with miscarriage at Risen Motherhood. Your foresight and care opened the door for me to process and share, and God has used it to bear fruit in many lives.

Paul David Tripp — Thank you for your constant support and encouragement in my life and ministry. I'm beyond grateful for your friendship.

www.ingramcontent.com/pod-product-compliance
Lightning Source LLC
Chambersburg PA
CBHW020546080526
44583CB00013B/1017